CW01582573

We Must be Sick (Mafia)

Elise Thornton

Copyright © 2024 by Elise Thornton

All rights reserved.

No portion of this book may be reproduced in any form without written permission from the publisher or author, except as permitted by U.S. copyright law.

Contents

1. Chapter 1 1
2. Chapter 2 5
3. Chapter 3 10
4. Chapter 4 14
5. Chapter 5 17
6. Chapter 6 20
7. Chapter 7 25
8. Chapter 8 29
9. Chapter 9 33
10. Chapter 10 36
11. Chapter 11 39
12. Chapter 12 44
13. Chapter 13 50
14. Chapter 14 56

15. Chapter 15 58
16. Chapter 16 62
17. Chapter 17 68
18. Chapter 18 72
19. Chapter 19 76
20. Chapter 20 80
21. Chapter 21 84
22. Chapter 22 86
23. Chapter 23 89
24. Chapter 24 93
25. Chapter 25 96

Chapter 1

I pushed my lunchbox away and leaned my head on my blond best friends shoulder."Want my chicken tenders?" I whispered "Yeah." He grabbed my lunchbox and took them out. He was building something with fries and nuggets.

"I think we should go back to Savanah." The boy twin spoke up"Excuse me?" I sat up"Are we just supposed to stay stuck then?" The boy asked"I'd rather be semi-stuck then permanently stuck." My sister rolled her eyes"If you and your dumb sister would have told us the truth from the beginning maybe we wouldn't be stuck at all." He sighed"I already told you why we didn't. I swear if you call her dumb again!" Ashlyn yelled a bit"Your one to talk. You brushed it off as a prank and walked off. If they told you would you have even believed them?" Aiden rubbed my back

"With your personality I seriously doubt it."

SLAM

"Whether I believed it or not THEY SHOULD HAVE TOLD US! NOW WERE STUCK IN SOME DEMONIC DIMENSION EVERY NIGHT RUNNING FROM FLESH EATING MONSTERS!IVE LOST COUND ON HOW MANY TIMES WE HAVE ALMOST DIED! NONE OF US HAVE SLEPT IN DAYS AND WE CANT TELL ANYONE AN-" He was cutoff by Ben slamming his fist onto the table. We kept talking about the subject.

~~Do we risk it?~~

Two weeks ago

Ashlyn was dancing while I was getting ready for s chool."Hey Troopers the bus-" My dad stopped because my sister fell "Don't." She glared at him"Oh yeah, the bus is down the street." He finished"NO IM NOT DONE LACING MY COMBAT BOOTS!" I yelled. Ashlyn hadn't even got dressed.

We both finished what we were doing and ran downstairs. I grabbed my tea while Ashlyn grabbed her coffee."BYE MOM!" We yelled in sync"BYE GIRLS!" She yelled back

We got on the bus.

Why is it so loud...

I was in front of Ashlyn cause I got on before her. There was an empty seat in front of a blond boy and a brown haired boy.

Shoot we made eye contact

As soon as Ashlyn sat down (she always wants the window seat) I sat beside her and the blond boy popped his head up."Hi!" He put his face close to mine. I jumped backwards. I got a really good look at him."AIDEN!?" I yelled"Y/N?!" He yelled back. We were both smiling."YOU DIDNT TELL ME YOU WERE MOVING HERE!" I sat upright "I DIDNT KNOW YOU LIVED HERE!" He was still grinning. I met Aiden when we were younger, about eight I'd say. I was playing on my parents phone and accidentally called a random number.

That random number was Aiden's mom's phone that he just happened to be on.

We talked on and off but then it became our daily thing.

"Soooo what's with the bus graveyard?" He asked"Just a junkyard with used busses." I smiled"That's it?" He asked"Yup." I answered "That's disappointing. I was hoping for some kind of lore or paranormal jazz." He did jazz hands then leaned back in his seat

It was quiet

"So that's Ben." My best friend pointed to him. I nodded. That's his cousin that got his vocal cords damage d...

We got off the bus and the blond would. Not. Be. Quiet. I know he's my best friend but my head is killing me...

"Woah. This is a small school." He was pulled back by Ben who pointed to the principals office. "We gotta pick our schedules- up" he stopped"Oh wow. They're fast." He started laughing.

Chapter 2

"INCOMING!" Someone yelled as a shoe almost took off my sisters head. Kids started yelling then randomly fighting. Welcome to high school...

A light brown haired boy dropped a paper and my sister picked it up"Here.""Oh- thanks!"

A puppy?

We have assigned seats...

I looked at who would be sitting behind me. HES GONNA KICK ME ALL DAY ISNT HE- the name tag had in bold letters "Aiden C."

"WE WOULDNT BE LATE IF YOU HELPED INSTED OF RECORDING!""Sorry we're late!" "Don't mark us tardy!""They aren't here yet.""We still have a chance!"

"A chance? Are two of my students late on the first day...just kidding! If you get here before me than your s- where's your shoe..." "You should find that after cla ss.""Yes sir."

I watched as the cousins walked in and the blond one had the biggest grin on his face. I just put my head down. As soon as he sat down I felt him push on the back of my seat.

"My name is Thomas Walter and this is my first time teaching my own class." The teacher wrote his name on the board "Ashlyn Banner, I like dogs." My sister sat down

"Y/N Banner. I like Kick-boxing and dance. Yes by the way, we are twins." I sat back down

"Aiden Clark, I like bungee jumping, skydiving, rock climbing, water skiing-" he was cut off by the teacher.

Ben was asleep. Honestly...mood.

"Hello I- the- uh... Logan Fields. I mean- I'm Logan...I enjoy astrology." He sat down

"I'm Taylor Hernández. I'm in the mechanics club. Come say hi if you get a chance!" She sat

"Im Tyler Hernández, yes, we're twins. I'm in the baseball club." He sat. I tuned out everyone else because my head was hurting.

Blah blah blah...semester long project...Blah...Group s...Blah...Cant work alone...Blah Blah...get with your groups.

I sat between Ashlyn and Aiden. They started talking about things and exchanging numbers. I didn't need Aiden's or Ashlyn's since I already had them.

"You two gonna go on the field trip?" Aiden asked"We'd rather stay home." I walked out. He looked like I had just kicked his puppy.

Time skip

"Looks like school went well." Mom ate another chip"It didn't." Ashlyn started whining about being in class with Aiden"On the bright side maybe you'll both make some friends. Y/N other than Aiden." Mom smiled"That isn't going to happen." Me and Ashlyn both glared at her

"HOW CAN YOU SAY THAT? HOW CAN YOU DEPRIVE YOUR PARENTS LIKE THIS!?" Mom yelled. I got a chair and hopped up to where I could hang by my legs on the bar that my parents installed on the ceiling.

"WHERE ARE THEY? OUR MEMORIES OF YOU HAVING SLEEPOVERS OR BIRTHDAY PARTIES!?" Mom yelled

"OUR MEMORIES OF BONDING WITH YOUR FRIENDS PARENTS! WE WANT THOSE PARENT-HOOD EXPERIENCES WHERE WE PRESS A GLASS TO YOUR DOOR AT 3AM TO LISTEN TO WHAT YOU AND YOUR FRIENDS TALK ABOUT!" Dad shouted

"You guys done?" Ashlyn rose an eyebrow"Yeah." Mom smiled

Knock

Knock

"I'll get it." Dad stood up. I was still hanging up-side down. "WAIT NO DONT OPEN THE D-" Ashlyn yelled

"Oh, Hi." I couldn't see him but I knew exactly who it was

Ashlyn ran upstairs

Aiden was legit trying to pull me off the bar"COME ONNNNNNN!" He shouted "AIDEN JUST LET ME HANG!" I was holding my shirt up"NOoOoOoOoOoOoOoOoOoOo!" He kept trying to pull me. I let go of my shirt and gave him my hands so he could pull me off."Finally." He smiled. Well, he's always smiling so...

Our parents kept talking and Aiden started talking about the field trip. So that's why he came over.

Time skip

Aiden handed me the pink paper then proceeded to crush me in a hug. "Please change your mind." He whispered "I might." I hugged back then they went home.

I walked upstairs and sat on mine and Ashlyn's shared bed. She came up not to long after. Dad started talking about how we should go.

Time skip

"I'm so glad you decided to come!" Aiden yelled"Aiden when are you gonna understand your loud voice hurts my ears?" I sighed"Sorry." He got on the bus behind me. I sat beside the window and Aiden sat beside me.

Chapter 3

The bus started moving. "Want one?" Aiden held up a rubix cube"Im not a big puzzle person." I shook my head no"Actually, I'll try." I put my hand out and he gave it to me. It was actually pretty easy to solve.

I leaned on his shoulder. "Tired?" He put his arm around my shoulder "Mhm." I hummed in response

Aiden POV

Awww she's so pretty...

I tucked her hair behind her ear. The way the light hits her face makes her look like an angel...

I closed my eyes and laid my head on top of hers

Y/N POV

I slowly opened my eyes letting them adjust to the light"We're here." Aiden looked down at me and grinned

Everyone walked out of the bus. Me and Ashlyn stretched. "Banner, you comin?" Aiden tugged at my shirt"Yeah, sorry." I started walking with the group while we debated what to do.

We ate then went on a horse ride."Will you two get down!?" Tyler yelled"Nope!" I smiled from the tree me and Aiden were sitting in. I didn't smile very much so it was kinda weird. "WE ARE IN A GRAVEYARD GET DOWN!" Tyler yelled again"Fine." I jumped out of the tree and started walking

We went to a light shop. Aiden put his head in a light and I took a photo.

"This face paint is pretty cute..." I looked over at my twin who also had while music notes on her face. Aiden was stealing coins so I just rolled my eyes.

~~This... Isn't as bad a I thought it would be~~

We started to walk back when a woman stopped us"Excuse me would you like a tour of the Sorrel weed h ouse...a group canceled a tour last minute so now we have some spots open. It's only five dollars." A girl with short black hair said"GUYS THIS PLACE IS REALLY HAUNTED! LETS GO!" Taylor smiled"I'm up for whatever." I crossed my arms.

"Right this way!" The woman smiled. That smile is eer ie...I don't like it.

They are just phantom noises they'll go away...

"Sis, you okay?" Ashlyn grabbed my hand"I'm fine..." I reassured her but she was not buying it.

I ignored everything the woman said. I know this woman is trouble. Plus, she just left so I mean hones tly...

We started walking around and the noises got louder. I looked in a room and saw a tall dark figure with white eyes and a creepy smile.

Nope...NOPENOPENOPE I DIDNT SIGN UP FOR THIS!

I took my earplugs out"Whys she wearing earplugs?" Tyler asked"Oh, I thought they were wireless earbuds!" Aiden yelled"Aiden they are for my sensitivity to...so unds..." I stared at the same figure I saw in that room except it was now at the end of the hall"Oop my bad." He covered his mouth

I froze. Ashlyn apparently saw it too. Are we both hall ucinating...?

"Are you two okay?" Taylor asked"We're fine." Ashlyn grabbed my hand. I squeezed hers.

"Why are you guys so quiet all the sudden?" That's when I felt it. I felt something cold touch my cheek.

Chapter 4

I closed my eyes as I felt Ashlyn squeeze my hand tighter. She yanked us both to the side and I felt my cheek get sliced

Shift

My body felt weird. When did it get behind us?

I put my hand up to my cheek. Nothing. It burns but there is no blood. Not even a trace of a cut. Tyler started yelling about it being some kind of prank then dragged Taylor out.

"Ya good?" Aiden put his hand on my head"Just spook ed..." I looked up at him

Time skip

I was laying in the hotel bed. It was big enough for three people so me, Taylor, and Ashlyn were all gonna sleep together. I think it's a queen...

Eventually Ash came in and not too much later Tay did too. We all talked about if we thought it was real or not.

I closed my eyes and fell asleep.

"/N. Hey, Y/N were in Savannah let's go." Aiden shook me. When did I fall asleep?"Okay." I grabbed my backpack.

Wait...w⊠ ⊠⊠⊠⊠⊠⊠⊠ ⊠⊠⊠ ⊠ff ⊠⊠⊠ ⊠⊠⊠ ⊠⊠ ⊠⊠v⊠⊠⊠⊠⊠...

I started walking around.

Ohhh this must be a dream. I'd probably be weird not to dream after what happened today. I don't think it's a nightmare...

I heard a noise

Shift

Now im on the bus...Ugh lucid dreams. They feel so real...

I slapped myself "Why did that kinda hurt..."

Yank

"Hey!" I yelled "What the..." I looked down. It was the thing from the Sorrel weed house.

I yanked myself up and fell out of bed"Sis...you okay?" Ashlyn asked"Yeah. Sorry." I felt something on my leg"What happened to your cheek?" She asked. Maybe I'm not awake...

I lifted up the blanket

Aiden POV

"Anyone else hear a scream?" I asked

WHAM

"TAYLOR!" Tyler ran out of his room and hit me in the face with his door"What's with the screaming? And what happened to your face?" Logan asked

"Ow" was all I said. We all chased after Tyler out the door.

Chapter 5

Y/N POV

"Taylor!" The door to our hotel room swung open"Tyler!" Taylor yelled"Oh, it's them. Why are they running?" Aiden asked"Something's in the..." Ashlyn looked back"Where's Y/N?" Aiden asked"She was right there!" Ashlyn yelled. I could hear their voices but for where I was at...come look in our room and find out.

"ASHLYN!" I screamed "IM COMING!" She yelled back. I could hear footsteps. The figures claw dug into my leg and I screamed again.

I saw the red head run in. She threw a lamp at the thing, helped me up and we ran as fast as we could. By the time we got out the door I was panting like a dog.

Ashlyn sat me down and I leaned against the wall." What was that?" Logan asked"According to Tyler that would be the "prank" from earlier." Aiden said while kneeling down beside me. The door started to open but Ben grabbed the handle."That could have been bad. Hahaha." Aiden laughed "COULD'VE? THE SKY IS RED FOR CRYING OUT LOUD!" Tyler yelled and I covered my ears.

"Guys...look down..." Taylor looked mortified. Aiden helped me stand. There were more of the things...and they were charging right at us. "How far is your room?" Ashlyn asked"Five or six door down." Aiden answered

"Aiden, give me the string from your shorts." Ashlyn started to untie her own"Kay. Why?" He started to untie his"I have an idea." She pulled the string out

She explained the plan and of course Tyler commented on it. Tyler, Logan, and Taylor all ran. I got on Ben's back because he's gonna carry me to the other room.

Ashlyn tied it and we ran. The string snapped almost immediately "AIDEN, BEN! MOVE!" Ashlyn yelled. They moved and Ashlyn slammed the cart into the thing. I got off Ben's back. "Ya know..." Aiden grabbed a spray bottle and pressed it to its head"This could be fun!" He grinned.

Chapter 6

Aiden sprayed the thing"Why isn't it screaming?" Aiden asked. I covered my ears. I was leaned against the balcony."We can take em! There are more bottles and-" he was cutoff by me grabbing his arm. He scooped me up bridal style and we started running.

We made it into the room then pushed the couch against the door. I sat in a corner with Aiden, Ben, and Ash. Aiden was laughing."Why are you laughing this time?" Tyler asked"It's like we're in a zombie movie." Aiden laughed more"That's funny?" Tyler said with an annoyed tone of voice "Yeah!" Aiden yelled a bit

"Your face is scratched." Aiden looked at me and tilted his head "I also have a gaping hole in my ankle, thanks for noticing." I groaned

"WAIT! YOU TWO KNEW IT WAS REAL AND DIDNT SAY ANYTHING!?" Tyler yelled"We didn't tell anyone because we didn't think it was real. And right now we should be coming up with a plan or something not arguing." Ashlyn looked at him"Why should we listen to anything you say? This is all probably your fault anyway." Tyler glared at her. Ashlyn went to stand up but I held her down and stood up inside. I limped over to Tyler.

"Alright fine. I get where you're coming from we should have said something. And if blaming us makes you feel better than do that." I grabbed his shirt "HEY WHAT ARE YOU-"

"If you aren't going to help the group Tyler, if you are going to keep insulting me and my sister then I will throw you to them. And if you're not gonna be useful... make yourself scarce. You can play the blame game after we're all safe. Those things can kill us at any moment. Who's your only source of ears here? That's right. Me and Ashlyn. Can you hear them? No, no you can't. So help come up with a plan." I let go of his shirt "Or keep your DUMB mouth ~~shut.~~" I smiled then limped back over to where I was sitting.

"That's my girl." Aiden whistled

Time skip

Ben poured alcohol on my ankle and I bit my hand.

SMASH

"Aye! Look another weapon!" Aiden yelled"Watch it! You should have done that in the bathroom cause now there's glass everywhere." Tyler glared at him"I-I'll get the broom..." Logan stood. I looked over at Tyler. Was that to harsh...

Ben rubbed a cotton ball on the hole and I flinched. Aiden walked over and gave me his hand. "You're just making more parts on your body bleed." He wiped my now bleeding hand on his shirt and put it in his. I squeezed his hand while Ben wrapped my ankle.

"I thought you'd be the leader." He rubbed my hand with his thumb "Our parents are both from the military so I try. Ash is more fit though. I can drive better than her and I can fight better than her but that's about the only two things I CAN do better than her. Plus, I don't even have my license." I sighed.

Ashlyn has always been better at everything. She probably will be.

"Ben, you're good at this. Thanks." I moved my ankle a little bit"Yeah, he's used to patching me up." Aiden let go of my hand. Ben started cleaning them wrapping that."From?" I knew he did dumb stuff but honestly he never really talked about personal life"Mm, a bunch of reasons. Skateboarding, rock climbing, hiking, jumping off of tall things. Stuff like that." He tilted his head"Ben, I'll do her face." He took the first aid kit. Ben honestly looked scared.

He started to clean the scratch on my face.

After he finished he got back up"How many of these do we have?" Ashlyn asked while picking up a chair leg"Eight, including the ones we're talking off." Taylor replied "It's been quiet for a while now. Do you think they're gone?" Taylor asked"Nope. Still there." I looked over at her "How do you know?" Tyler asked

"Like I said earlier. Me and Ashlyn can hear them. It's not really normal. We told you we had sensitive ears at that place we first saw it. They make a certain noise. The thing is, due to our condition we hear phantom noises, noises that aren't there. In the Sorrel weed house I heard the noises and at first just thought the thing was a hallucination." I stopped"But then it grabbed us." Ashlyn finished

"A hallucination grabbed you and you thought it wasn't real?" Tyler scoffed "You said it was a prank and- nevermind what I'm getting at is that me and her can hear them while you can't." Ashlyn was hitting herself with the pole. Probably trying to not hit Tyler because I REALLY wanna hit him too.

Chapter 7

"So your gonna use your magic hearing to save the day?" Tyler asked"No- well...yes but not right now. We should stay here for now that way we can prepare ourselves for later. Once we go outside we don't know what's gonna happen. We don't wanna be split up." Ashlyn managed to calm Tyler down"There's not much we can do so try mental exercises." Ashlyn suggested "Mental exercises?" Aiden asked"Imagining yourself in situations to see how you'll react. Anytime you're not asleep try them." Ashlyn stood"Great. Day-dream and hope we don't die from monsters." Tyler was at it again

"Is it still twelve?" Ashlyn asked logan"Yeah..." He replied

Shift

I sat up and looked at Ashlyn. It hurts but I feel no bandages and my hand has no marks...

Was that all a nightmare or am I still dreaming

"Are we in the bed?" Taylor gasped"WHERES THE OTHERS ARE THE MONSTERS STILL-" She stopped "SO IT DID HAPPEN! YOU REMEMBER RIGHT?" I shook her

We ran into the bathroom and started throwing our guts up"Are you guys okay...?" The girl we were sharing the room with asked "Found em!" Aiden yelled"Wait. ..Ain't you supposed to be dead?" Aiden looked at the girl"Move." Tyler shoved him

"Haha...I feel another wave coming on..." Aiden stumbled over to me

Just what...is going on. I felt someone rub my back as I threw up again."Thanks Aiden..." I mumbled

Present time

"Alright. We can take a group vote tonight." Ashlyn finally gave in. "Why not after school?" Tyler asked"Me and Y/N have ballet later." Ashlyn answered"Just skip it." Tyler shrugged"Uh...Ty, we have stuff to do too." Taylor nudged him"I help with the flower shop today." Logan whispered

"Even with what's happening, you can't just neglect things that will help us in the future." Taylor yelled a bit"WE ARENT GOING TO HAVE A FUTURE IF WERE DEAD!" Tyler yelled"Tyler, it's not just about our future. Do you think that's really what we're worried about? We need to survive and the world does most certainly not revolve around you. We're gonna end up in a Psyche-ward." I glared at him

"She does have a point. We're what people call crazy." Aiden spun his finger

"Whatever." Tyler stomped off. He spun around, glared at us, grabbed Taylor and stomped off again.

Time skip

"Aiden do you ever take your contacts out?" I asked"When I sleep yeah." He slouched in his seat as the bus stopped"Whatcha doin?" I asked as I stood up"I wanna get off here." Aiden smiled "Aiden I leave in an hour." I glared at him"If there is an emergency I wanna know where to go." He shrugged

We all walked in"Oh, Aiden and Ben are over? You have ballet today." Mom looked up"Yeah. They wanna see where the studio is." I took my shoes off. Mom and dad pulled me and Ash over the couch and asked if they were forcing us.

"Whatcha talking bout?" Aiden asked

...Silence...

"Sorry, got bored waiting." He stood up.

Chapter 8

"Momma I'm ready. Can you do my hair?" I walked down the stairs. I had changed into a tank top and stretchy shorts.

Okay they were worried about them bullying me now they are playing cards together...traitors

"Sure!" She smiled. I walked down and sat between her legs. She pulled my hair up into a bun then we got in the car. It was crammed since it was only meant for three people.

Me and Ashlyn shared a seat.

Aiden laid his head on my shoulder."We're here." Mom and dad looked back. "Woah! This place is cool!" Aiden grinned"Satisfied?" Ashlyn asked"Yup!...Actually, can we come I-" he was cutoff by Ashlyn slamming the door"NO!" She yelled

Taylor POV

"Tyler...?" I looked up at him"Sorry." He sighed and sat down"We can't keep skipping..." I looked at the floor"Yeah yeah, I know. I need baseball to get into college and your mechanics club has connections I get it. I just- does it matter if we die?" He asked"You just wanna throw all our hard work away...all our plans?" I asked"I didn't- things just had to become more complicated didn't they." He got under the blanket

Logan POV

Five more hours...

"Logan?" My grandpa shouted a bit"Y-Yeah?" I looked at him"You alright son? You look a little clammy." He looked me up and down"Y-Yeah! I'm fine!" I smiled "He's looked clammy for the past couple weeks. Ever since he went on that field trip then quit astronomy club. Something's wrong. You know you can tell us anything." My grandma healed up a tool

"I'm fine I swear! You don't need to worry." I looked at the plants"Woah...these need watered." I turned the hose on

Aiden POV

"BEN SHES MY BEST FRIEND! HOW DO I TELL HER!?" I yelled. He rolled his eyes and started writing again."Just do it. She'll understand." Is what he wrote "Ben this could break our friendship...it- it- this could break us!" My voice cracked. He started writing again. "Let it out." He held his arms out and I hugged him

"I just wanna tell her...I wanna tell her everything." I started crying

Ashlyn POV

I laid down and looked at Y/N

"You only do that when you're sad or on your period and I know it's not the second one. What's wrong." I stared at her as she cuddled with the plushie Aiden had bought and shipped here a while back"Ash...how do you confess?" She asked"HOLD UP WHAT?" I yelled a bit causing her to cover her ears

"I like Aiden." She rolled over to face me. The plushie was pressed against her chest and her cheeks were pink. "AWWEEEEEEE!" I hugged her. I hated lovey dovey stuff but just this once...this one time...I actually think it's cute

We both got under the covers and midnight slowly creeped up on us"Sis...the phantom is still the-" I was cutoff

Y/N POV

I shoved Aiden off of me with my bloody hand"Duck." Ashlyn got down behind a seat and so did everyone else "What do we do?" Taylor whispered "We have to kill it." I waved my hand"How?" Tyler asked"Logan can shoot it through the window." Aiden suggested "The gun is for emergency's only." Ashlyn rolled her eyes"This is an emergency!" Tyler whisper yelled"A emergency is a swarm on one of us is about to-" She was stopped by my hand covering her mouth

We all got under the seats.

Chapter 9

I looked forward just to be met with the phantoms face. It swung its hand at Ashlyn and grabbed her braid. I rotated myself and kicked its arm.

It grabbed me and started to pull me"Not good!" Tyler yelled. It shoved all of its claws into my leg.

I screamed

"No! NO STOP!" It bit me. What is this thing, a zombie!? I tried kicking it with my other foot but it just dug its claws into that one too.

"STOP IT!" I screamed. Aiden pulled me up while the phantom still a hold on my legs. He pushed its head down and it pulled its claws out. Aiden moved me to the front of the bus. I sat in his lap shaking."Hey, hey your okay." He cradled me. I cried. "Hey, shhhh it's okay. It's okay wise girl..." He held my face against his chest. He was shaking too.

Tyler grabbed the phantom and swung it around. He laid back in a seat and threw it over him."CLOSE THE WINDOW!" He yelled. It swung at Logan but it missed. Ben stabbed it. I couldn't see what happened after that because I had my face buried in Aiden's chest.

I heard them running. "Is she okay?" Tyler asked"Does she LOOK okay to you?" Aiden snapped at him. I looked up at them. He wasn't smiling. He was crying."Ben can you patch her up please..." Aiden stood up. I grabbed his arm.

They moved me to the floor. I laid my head on Aiden's lap and gave him both my hands. I was gonna try to to kick Ben.

He looked at me. I nodded. "OKAY THAT STINGS A LOT WORSE!" I screamed. They couldn't find the pain killers. I squeezed Aiden's hands. He was back to that fucking grin. Aiden let one of my hands go and put his hand on my cheek. He stroked it with his thumb while I was pretty much resting the urge to kick Ben in some not nice places.

"Are you done?" I looked at my now bandaged legs. Ben nodded."Thanks..." I closed my eyes and fell over.

Chapter 10

I opened my eyes"Guys?" I looked out in the isle "SHES AWAKE!" Aiden ran over and hugged me"Uhhhh how do I walk?" I asked"Oh..." Taylor walked over and sat beside me"I can carry you." Aiden smiled"Alright." I smiled

Tyler and Ashlyn started arguing we decided to take a vote. We decided to wait one year.

They went and dug up a white board "This is our first goal." She started writing "How do we do that?" Tyler asked

First main objective:Gun shop

"We need better weapons." Ashlyn put the lid on the market"How do we do that?" Tyler asked again "Well, first we need to do two things."

-Fortify graveyard walls-Bring jeep into graveyard

"As we know injury's heal faster here. Well wait till Y/N is healed since she can drive best out of us all." Ashlyn looked over at me"My parents jeep is the closest to the graveyard so that's the car we can use." She paused"Does anyone have any ideas on how to fortify the walls?" She asked. Ben drew the wall with barbed wire.

"That might work if they were regular humans." Tyler said pointing out the fact that they could climb them"Oh yeah. Good try Ben." Taylor hugged him

"Since they don't react well to light, would light fixtures work?" Aiden asked "Not to sure if the generator has enough power...most of the power goes to the door so if they went off when we opened the door what's the point?" Ashlyn answered

"Some solar lights.""Oh yeah, that would work." "How do we get them?"

"Oh, leave that to me! I've been saving up my allowance for a while now." Aiden pointed at himself "Allowance? how much do you have?" "Uhm about _." Aiden answered

"Anyway...I have a card so I can order them and have them shipped here." Aiden tilted his head "Oh yeah, Aiden can I have your knife?" Ashlyn asked

"Yeah wh-" He stopped "These need to go." Ashlyn cut her braids"Ash, can you cut mine?" I asked"Mhm." She knelt behind me and I felt the weight of my braids go away.

Time skip

Me and Ashlyn both looked at our shadows."Huh...t hat's weird." She held her braids up. She helped me up."How are your legs?" She asked"They hurt. I think I can walk." I stood up and kinda had to shimmy to the closet.

Time skip

Aiden POV

"Can you order those lights during lunch?" Ashlyn asked"Yeah." I replied "Where's Y/N?" Taylor asked"I don't know. She walked off when we got to school." Ashlyn shrugged

"Found her." Tyler looked up from her phone. My eyes widened as I looked up and saw what was happening.

Chapter 11

"Okay is she being bullied?" Ashlyn asked"Oh...it's him. And he's after Y/N and Logan!" Taylor rolled her eyes"On it." Tyler started to walk

Y/N POV5 minutes earlier

"Barron for the last time. We are done doing your homework!" I yelled. He slapped me across the face."Who said you could talk, Dog?" Barron asked. Logan flinched when I was slapped.

"At least leave Logan out of it."

Slap

"Talking out of turn again? Do you need taught a lesson?" He started to press one of his knees against my leg. He figured out they were hurting because of how I was walking."Stop." Logan glared at him

Slap

"Your talking too?" He asked while grinning. I was clearly in pain

"Yeah yeah I'll take care of it." I looked over.

Thank god...

I saw the way Ben looked and mouthed 'Calm down. I'll be okay.' Aiden jumped in front of him"Barron, what are you doing?" Tyler asked. He stopped putting pressure on my leg

"Oh great...Just talking to my science partners about the project." Barron didn't even look at him"I'm sure you were." Tyler looked over at us"I'm not an idiot Barron. We could hear you from the end of the hall. Your skating on thin ice with coach so how would he feel if you were treating your 'partners' like this?" Tyler glared at him"So annoying...fine." Barron walked away

"Thanks..." Logan mumbled"You're scared of him, after all those nights with those things?" Tyler asked sounding annoying "That's pathetic." He finished

"Tyler, LAY OFF!" I yelled"What was that about?" Taylor asked"We didn't do his part of the project." I mumbled

We started talking about asking mine and Ashlyn's parents teaching us self defense.

Class passed by really fast.

"Am I seeing this right?" Tyler asked"Woah, that's pretty rad." Aiden grabbed one of my braids "Let go before I brake your arm." I glared at him"This might have something to do with how injuries pass over from this dimension but not the phantom dimension." Logan looked down at the show again "Speaking of injuries, how are you holding up?" Ashlyn asked"Oh um...it's sore. It kinda feels like I've been doing sit ups or so mething..." Logan held his side "About you guys, what happened?" Ashlyn asked"Oh- about that. Ya sure you wanna tell them?" Aiden asked while looking at Ben "It's best to have these things out in the open if we're gonna be a team." A robotic voice said. Ben put his earbuds in and sat beside me. I nodded and smiled.

"Alright, that's that then." Aiden shrugged and sat on the other side of me"He's probably right though, that way you don't say him off or somethin." He rolled his shoulders "Set him off?" Ashlyn asked"Yeah. But...this conversation doesn't go outside this group. You got it?" He glared at everyone except me and Ben. "Okay." Everyone said except Tyler"Don't tell me what to do-ow." He stopped because Taylor punched him.

"I don't know if you guys have noticed yet but Ben has like extreme anger issues. Much worse than the half-wit over there. And- this also has to do with the reason he doesn't speak. Ben was in sixth when the incident happened. Or was it seventh- anyway, he's always been a big guy for his age and it tended to intimidate people. Despite his appearance though, he was pretty timid. And more than anything...he loved singing. It was everything to him. However, since it didn't match his personality people started to make fun of him for it." He paused. I rubbed Ben's back. I've know this since it happened... Aiden started talking again"It's didn't start as bullying. At first the offered to 'fix' him. Offering that if he'd join their group they would tech them how to fight. After Ben refused well, that's when it started. They started beating him every day. Afterwards the leader, Shane, would ask Ben to join the group, and every time...Ben said no. That was until one day Shane decided to take it to a drastic level."

Chapter 12

In the words of Red, this episode has violence some may find disturbing.

"Shane strangled Ben. Not with the intent to kill him, but enough to damage Ben's voice box. All because he knew singing was something precious to Ben. Afterwards Ben started spiraling into depression and then depression turned to rage. When Ben finally went back to school he confronted the group." He stopped to breathe for a second. I looked at Ben and sure enough he had his head down. I ran my hand over his and he grabbed mine.

"But even after he beat the ones who hurt them he didn't feel any better. He didn't know what to do...to make the anger go away. So he kept picking fights, even street fights. He stopped going to school and even started coming home late. His parents didn't know what to do. Ben refused to go to therapy and would sneak out. At some point, he fought a kid whose big brother had connections with a gang. The gang found where he lived and well...They had to move." He stopped to breathe. I squeezed Ben's hand.

"Ben was ashamed of what happened and realized his temper was out of control. Then his parents suggested he come stay with us. Since we're always traveling and moving they thought it would help him find a new meaning in life. Something he loved as much as singing. And he started to go to therapy. And so that's how he ended up with me. His therapist also suggests calm things like gardening, and drawing. That's why he always has that notebook. He's calmed down quite a bit but things still trigger him. When he moved in with me Y/N knew sign language and he took it up so they could talk without him having to write. She's a big part in calming him down." Aiden looked over at me. I smiled.

"Alright Ben...We're done." I signed. He pulled his earbuds out and signed "ok"

"Alright let's move on then..." Ashlyn was cutoff by Taylor"Thank you Ben. For letting Aiden tell us that I mean- you don't even know us that well but felt like we should know as a team. I'm sure that wasn't easy. I just wanted to let you know it was appreciated" Taylor smiled. Ben blushed and nodded. I let go of his hand.

"Oh- sorry for interrupting you Ashlyn..." "No, it's fine. I also agree it was nice to have let us know.""M-Me too." "Yeah."

"Uhm this is a little off topic, but I think I have a theory of what happened in Savannah." Logan spoke up"Well er- not exactly what happened but how we went from Savannah Georgia, all the way back here to Alto, Georgia on the second night." He put his hands up a bit"Right...that's something we've been stuck on a while." Ashlyn mumbled. I thought back to the second night. Yeah, that was awful...

"Okay so what's the theory?" Tyler asked"Well, because of how our injuries work in relation to the dimensions, I think our bodies here are connected to the phantom realm ones but at the same time...not. So if they are connected in some way...what if there's a distance limit?" Logan looked up"Like, if you travel to far from one body the other resets its position instead of going to where it was previously." He interlocked his hands

"That would make sense. How far is the distance limit though...and, if we travel to far in the phantom dimension will our physical bodies go there?" Ashlyn asked. Aiden just looked like someone had told him the earth was flat. "That's a possibility...but there's still also the fact that things don't move the same in the phantom dimension as they do in the human. I'm not sure how to test it though..." Logan replied

Theory blah blah more theory blah blah

SLAM

I looked over at Aiden. Why did he just slam his head off the table-"I get that the phantom dimension is important but can we talk about something more exciting...?" He asked. Tyler stood up and raised his hand."Don't." Taylor held his other arm. Ashlyn looked over and rose her hand"Ash..." I grabbed her hand

"What do you think about asking my parents about self defense?" I asked"REALLY?" He yelled"Ah wait-YOUR HAIR!" He grabbed my shoulders"IF WE SHOWED YOUR PARENTS YOURS AND ASHLYNS

SHADOW WOULDNT THAT BE ENOUGH PROOF?" He asked still yelling "Aiden let go." I glared at him. He's right...that might be enough...

"Wow, he does have a brain." Tyler rolled his eyes "Good idea!" Taylor smiled"I said let go!" I pinched him"Rude!" He let go and laughed

Time skip

I sat on my front porch with Ash, Ben, and Aiden."So, do you know any moves?" I signed to Ben"Not really." He signed back"Oh, there they are." Aiden jumped off the railing. I looked back and saw the twins with Logan. "Tsk, you guys should really wear helmets." Aiden stuffed his hands in his pockets"Like you would." Tyler rolled his eyes"Tyler has a point." I shrugged"Mom, Dad?" Ashlyn shouted"Kitchen!" They yelled

"Uh what are you guys doing?" She asked"Making a snack platter...?" Mom smiled"I see that but you can't eat all that..." Ashlyn looked at the food"W-Well you and your friends usually go straight to the graveyard to hang out-" dad stuttered"-But you said you wanted to speak with us so...We made snacks to eat while we talk." mom finished. Were they really that excited...?

Smack

Smack

Chew

I glared at Aiden"Dude..." Tyler took the words right out of my mouth. I slapped his cheek and he looked over at me."Eat quieter AND CLOSE YOUR MOUTH!" I yelled"So...what do you kids wanna talk about?" Dad asked

That photo of Ashlyn and the phantom is so cool though.

Chapter 13

"Oh yeah." Ashlyn stood up and pulled me up with her. We walked over infront of the lamp."Do you notice anything about or shadows?" Ashlyn asked"Well uh- not particularly no..." dad tilted his head. "Are we supposed to notice something...?" Mom asked"Ah- nevermind forget about it." I sat back down."We do need your help." Ash sat down too"Logan is being bullied." I looked up. "So are you." Tyler pitched in"WHAT!? SINCE WHEN!? WHO?" Mom and dad yelled"Calm down..." I rolled my eyes"You are gonna tell us later. You got that." Dad narrowed his eyes"Yes." I nodded

"Okay as I was saying- that's why he has that bruise. Can you teach them self defense basics?" Ashlyn asked"Yeah...but are your parents okay with that?" Mom asked.

We were all silent. "Yeah- ask them first. We don't need any unnecessary drama when you guys go home with bruises." Dad looked at the floor. We all went out to the graveyard and started talking.

A month later

"UGH!" Tyler yelled as he fell. "Alright Logan, your up." Dad smiled"Your dad's brutal..." Tyler scratched the back of his neck "No one said it would be easy." Ashlyn looked at the ground

THUD

"Actually...I think I'm more scared of your mom and sister." He looked over at me"See Aiden, under like that. Also, thanks Tyler!" I let Aiden out of the headlock and stood up. "Alright, that should be a good stopping point." Mom got up and stretched. I pulled Aiden up. "Safe..." Logan sighed"DONT LET YOUR GAURD DOWN!" Dad put him in a head lock"You kids wanna come in and play some board games? We can make food." Mom stood infront of front of us"We can't...we gotta study for midterms." Taylor sighed"Oh, well...we 'll bring the food out to you!" Mom smiled and walked away with dad

"Haha that midterms joke was great." Aiden sat in a tire"It wasn't a joke. They are next week." Tyler looked down at him. I took out my earplug and Ashlyn did too."You hear that?" I asked"Yeah." She stood up and I did too. We started to walk."Huh- Ashlyn, Y/N?" Taylor watched us walk

"What's up did you hear something again?" Aiden and Tyler walked over"Yeah, but it's just a bird." Ashlyn answered "You got worked up over a crow?" Tyler asked"It sounded like footsteps." I looked back at him"Maybe you got it mixed with your parents walking away." Taylor reasoned"Nevermind...let's just finish with the traps." Ashlyn walked away but I stared at the crow.

"You okay?" Aiden asked"Hang on..." I walked over and looked under the car then the bus. "Y/N?" He followed me"Nevermind." I walked back to the rest of them

Time skip

I swung my legs while sitting between Aiden and Ash. I noticed my untied lace and pulled my foot up to tie my combat boot."This is definitely not what I was expecting." I looked out at all the phantoms and let my leg fall back down. We all climbed down off the wall.

"Alright, let's go over this one last time." Ashlyn crossed her arms"Um- guys are uh- are we sure we wanna do this?" Taylor asked"...what?" Ashlyn looked at her"I mean...Y'know maybe staying in the graveyard wouldn't be so bad right? With the lights we can hide till the seven hours are up." She looked up "I-I like that idea." Logan was pretty much clinging to the ladder."Are you serious? I thought you guys wanted out of here and now you're saying you don't minds being trapped for the rest of our lives?" She asked"And you- why are you being so quiet? You're the one who pitched a fit about wanting to go back." She glared at Tyler

"That was before we knew about the lights and BEFORE there was a giant horde of those things outside our door! I'm not saying we should stop trying to find a way out- maybe just not with this plan. We don't even need guns anymore right!?" Tyler yelled"And you chose to bring this up now?" Ashlyn ran her hand through her short hair. "After all the prepping,

The training,

The sneaking around placing traps,

And right before we actually do something, you wanna back out!?"

"There's to many right now!""That's why we have the traps!""No.""NO!""I AM GETTING THAT JEEP. EVEN IF WE DECIDE WE DONT NEED GUNS WELL EVENTUALLY NEED TO GET OUT OF HERE AND LEARN HOW THIS PLACE WORKS SO WE CAN ESCAPE!" She yelled"Ash maybe you should-""DONT TELL ME WHAT TO DO!" She yelled louder. I flinc hed."YOU ARE SO ANNOYING NOW! GOD, EVER SINCE WE WENT ON THAT DUMBASS TRIP YOU HAVE PUSHED MY BOUNDARIES! YOU ARE SO FUCKING CLINGY AND DUMB NOW!" She even louder.

"Oh, alright."

I walked over to the bus ladder and climbed it. It was silent now and no one was trying to stop me. I made it on top of the wall and just stared at the phantoms. "Wait Y/N please-" Taylor shouted "What?" I looked down at all of them"Come on- get down." Tyler looked up at me. I pulled my phone out and connected my earbuds to my phone. Then I turned on 'I think I'm okay' by YUNGBLUD

"What? Afraid I'm gonna jump?" I tilted my head. All their eyes widened and I walked backwards till I felt my foot meet the edge."DONT!" Ashlyn yelled"Thought I was dumb though? I'm gonna show you dumb." I turned around and faced the phantoms.

Chapter 14

I threw myself off the wall then spun midair so I'd land on my feet. I grabbed my knife out of my pocket and stared at the phantoms."Damn...there she is a lot of you." I smiled almost psychotically. I ran out of the light and heard various people screaming my name from the wall.

This is SICK!

I ran to the car and tugged on the handle. "Damn it..." I groaned and got on the roof of the car"ITS LOCKED!" I screamed. Despite me yelling that the music turned on and they threw the ropes over. Aiden jumped not even acknowledging the rope. The rest of them climbed down. Aiden ran to the car while grinning. When he got over he held his arms out and I jumped off the roof of the car into them.

"You really are dumb." He laughed"I know." I grinned. Everyone else made it over. Ashlyn and Tyler argued then we ran in the house. Aiden fell in front of me."Hey, what's wrong?" I looked down at him"Uhhhhh-" he lifted his pants leg"Pfttt from when you jumped?" I laughed"Y- WATCH OUT!" He yelled

I felt something grab the collar of my shirt and my head was banged against the roof. I felt the blood start to trickle down my face. Aiden tried to get up but just tripped "NO!" He yelled. From what I could see he was very much not smiling...

I tried to grab my knife but I couldn't.

I dropped it.

Chapter 15

I had dropped it.

I groaned as my light was pulled off my head and my hair was pulled. Did I pass out...?

I grabbed the phantoms wrist. I tried to pull back but I was slammed into the roof. Everything is spinning and I can't fight back...if I can make Logan an opening!

I punched it

It lifted its claw. Come on Logan! PLEASE! Tears threatened to spill as I was choked."Let me go!" I managed to choke out. It tilted its head and almost looked as if it understood."Please...I don't wanna die..."

BANG

It fell limp beside me. Logan thank you so much..."Y/N!" "Aiden...?" I tried to sit up"Your okay!" He stared down at me"Define okay...I think- no I have a concussion." I looked up at him"Here." He put his hand down and the phantom slipped. Its leg caught my pants and I started to slide.

He jumped over and used his pickaxe to hold us."I'm not letting you go this time." He pulled me up

"We need help..." he managed to drag me to the window. Taylor pulled me through and Tyler got me on his back. I could barely see. I looked out the window and saw a bunch of blurry figures running towards the house."L ovely..." I mumbled.

Tyler opened the door just to be met with a phantom. We both screamed and he jumped back. There was another phantom on the ceiling so I shined my flashlight at it. They started crawling through the window. "Guys, stay in a circle. Me and Aiden can cover the ceiling." I looked up. We started waking."You have actually got to be kidding me..." Tyler grumbled. The living room was full of them.

We slowly made it out of the house. Aiden grabbed me off Tyler's back and pulled me onto his lap as soon as he got in the car. Taylor started to drive and the windows shattered.

"Logan press the button!" It was Ash. The door opened and we drove in. I heard a slam signaling it was shut." Everyone okay?" Taylor asked. I got out of the car while trying to stand. Taylor grabbed me and held me upright while Tyler threw up."We did it." Taylor whispered "WE DID IT!" She held the keys up."Yeah, we're pretty great huh." Tyler smiled

"Logan...that was awesome." I was breathing heavy but managed to smile"N-no you guys did most of the work." He shook his head"Stop. You've barely had any experience with a gun besides Aiden's airsoft and I doubt that comes anywhere near the real thing. Be proud." Tyler laughed

Without Logan...no... without them I would be dead on that roof right now.

"We should celebrate!" Aiden shouted"Y/N you okay? You haven't talked. Do you need to sit down?" Taylor asked"No. Im alright." I smiled and laughed

"Just a little...lightheaded is all." The ground got closer to my face and it all went dark

Three episodes in one now, let's admire this episodes art because it's so good I could eat it.

Chapter 16

"THAT WAS THE ELEVENTH TIME SHES ALMOST CAUGHT ME! WHAT KIND OF SUPER HEARING DOES SHE HAVE?!" I yelled"I CANT EVEN GET CLOSE TO THOSE TWO WITHOUT THEM ALMOST HEARING ME!""YESTERDAY WAS ANOTHER CLOSE CALL! AND THE RECORDING DEVICES ARE BUGGING OUT! ITS SO FRUSTRATING! WHY DO WE SNEAK AROUND!? WHY CANT WE JUST NAB THEM IF BOSS IS SO INTERESTED!?"

"Be patient Ryan. He said we need to lay low after the Savannah stunt. Both sides are trying to track us down." A cloaked man said

"IT MAKES NO SENSE! If things went how they usually go we wouldn't have popped up on their radars. All the kids should be at least comatose! Especially the twin girls! Right Jasmine?"

"You're getting annoying. How many times must I repeat myself? I led her to the rift, she interacted with it, I saw it physically open large enough to drag the other kids in too, then they walked out like nothing happened and the rift was completely closed."

"Not sure what boss thinks is 'interesting' or whatever's going on. That's why he's having you gather information. So if your devices aren't working then listen the old-school way."

"If boss thinks they're important, they must be important to the cause as well."

Y/N POV

Worst headache ever...

I stood up. I put on a tank top, a hoodie, and sandals.

"Mom, dad, I'm leaving. Love you bye." I opened the door"We love you!" Was all I heard then I shut the door. Me and Ashlyn still haven't spoke since last night...

I stared up at the spot my head was hit off of. Why did the phantom not slash me...it had the chance but it didn't. Did it really understand me or am I overthinking?

Mom POV

"Hey Em, can you make us another pot of coffee for work?" Mike asked"Yeah. Dibs on the blue mug." I pulled my hair up.

I started to pour the coffee then I saw the...thing in the reflection. "What the..." I threw the pot

Thump

Thud

Thud

Thud

Thud

"EMMA!? ARE YOU OKAY?" Mike ran into the kitchen"Yeah, careful glass is everywhere." I groaned "Can you grab the broom?" I asked. We started to sweep the glass."It happened again?" He asked"...yeah." I closed my eyes"At this point maybe we should call an exorcist." He sighed"Well, seeing how these uh- incidents are happening more." He looked up at me

"I know you aren't gonna want to hear this but...do you remember when the girls were born?" Mike asked

"HUSH!" I yelled

"Emma...we both know that it looks similar. This might be the same thing." He grabbed my hand

Y/N POV

Today has been weird quiet..."You two are getting on my nerves." Tyler stopped walking"How are we supposed to 'celebrate' when you're ruining it with your awkwardness?" He asked"What Tyler means is you both seem a bit tense. There's about 10 minutes before class. You guys talk and we'll grab some snacks!" Taylor smiled

Me and Aiden just kinda stood there not saying anything "Are you sure you should have come today with your head like that?" He asked"What about you? You're limping." I crossed my arms"Yeah but- that's my fault." He laughed a little"Aiden we should talk later my heads throbbing." I looked out the window"Hang on..." he stepped towards me and slipped his hand in my hood onto the back of my head

"I'm really sorry Y/N." He whispered

"I didn't think me getting hurt would get you hurt.

Flashback

He pulled me up and hugged me"I'm sorry..." he whispered "Aiden right now isn't the time..." I stopped myself so I didn't hurt his feelings. He's shaking...is he scared?

Just...just for a second

I hugged him back

End of flashback

"Ah- sorry." He pulled his hand out"I'm still not used to the boundary thing. From where we only talked over the phone the only thing I wanted for years was to hug you..." he backed up a bit. I walked towards him and pulled him into a hug."Aiden...I don't blame you for what happened last night. You're my best friend and I won't blame you for anything you didn't do. Now about boundaries...just try your best okay. And learn to ask."

I smiled up at him. God I wish I could tell him how I feel...

"Okay!" He grinned and hugged back putting one hand on the back of my head gently.

Chapter 17

"Let's both try our best." I pulled away from the hug"Yeah." He shrugged

"Wow, that was cringy."

"Tyler? We can hear you." I rolled my eyes

Time Skip

"Im pretty sure I failed that midterm..." Tyler put his head in his hands. I think I did to...

"Oh yeah, my parents are coming home tomorrow." Aiden stuffed another cookie in his mouth. "Really?" Taylor asked"Yeah, I think it's Ben's little sisters birthday in a week." He looked at Ben and he nodded"Oh, they're coming back? They never told me." My dad looked up"You talk to them?" Ashlyn asked"Yeah, I talk to them about how Aiden and Ben are doing." He shrugged

"Should we have a barbecue?" Dad looked over"What?" I asked"It'll be a chance to know the other parents. We could have a barbecue to celebrate both birthdays." He nodded"What do you mean both?" Ashlyn asked. I sighed"Our birthday." I rolled my eyes"Yeah." Dad smiled. We all agreed about the barbecue. "Oh! You kids should probably leave soon. It's almost 5." Dad looked down at his watch

"You sure you don't want me to drive you?" Dad asked"Yeah, it's not a far walk. Plus the jeep doesn't have enough seats." Ashlyn rolled her eyes"Well actu ally...I made a small jeep upgrade."

I ran upstairs and stuffed my knife before running out to the car and sliding in beside Aiden. The upgrade was two seats in the back that the twins were crammed into.

"You kids have fun! Call me if you need anything" Dad smiled"We will!" Ashlyn waved"The arcade is fun and all but...are you two gonna be okay?" Taylor asked. I just nodded."Well, we've never been to an arcade so it might be fun." Ashlyn shrugged

We walked in and I looked at the DDR machines "Bet I can beat you." Aiden smirked "How much?" I smiled. Was that blush-"Oh! Oh! I'm pretty good at that too!" Taylor smiled "I-I know how but I'm not good." Logan smiled slightly

I stepped onto the machine and slid my hands onto the bars. I beat Aiden by a long shot.

We played basketball, hockey, a shooter game, then Ben did a strength game. "I think this is enough for decent prizes!" Taylor looked at Aiden who was buried in the tickets."I get all of Aiden's." I looked at the door"All of them!?" He whined

I tapped Logan's shoulder and he looked over. "Well that's annoying. Why is he here?" Tyler asked"Who-oh...Barron." Taylor scrunched her nose"Doubt he'll do anything." Tyler crossed his arms. Aiden covered Ben's face. "It's still weird..." Taylor picked the tickets up"Guys wait- that kid isn't a part of the group." I pointed"He used to do that to us all the time." Logan sighed"Wanna warn him...?" I asked. Logan nodded." Do what you need and we'll be with you." Tyler smiled

We walked out the doors"Woah- that caught me off guard. Four eyes? Demi?" Barron laughed. I cringed at the nickname Demi."It's been a while pal. How ya doin?" He asked. I looked over at Logan who was shaking.

"Remember...the phantoms are scarier." I whispered

That knife boutta get put to work.

Chapter 18

"My names Y/N. This here is Logan." I put my hand out "Oh...I'm Noah." The boy shook my hand"Is he making you do homework? You shouldn't have to do that." Logan held his hand out"H-He's not forcing me. He just asked and..." Noah was cutoff"And you felt guilty saying no." I crossed my arms"It's okay to help people just...stay away from people like Barron. It won't end well." I tried to reason"He has a tactic to prolong beating you into what he wants so it takes longer to get caught. If you keep working then...when you don't finish on time, bet below an 80, try to do your work before his, of upset him he-"

"Hey! Just what do you think you're doing? I leave you two alone and this is how you..." he was cutoff by Logan"See? This is how he normally acts. You'll feel awful if you stay." I moved my hands"You can come hang out with me and Logan or you can go home if you'd like! I just felt like we needed to warn you." I smiled and Barron walked over. He threw a punch but I dodged it easily

"Too slow"

He started poking Logan in the head"Your just a useless loser who's parents didn't even want him." Barron kept poking him till Logan slapped his hand away"I'm usel ess...when you refuse to do your own work? When you waste others time just to turn around and hurt them?" Logan looked and sounded different from normal "Not even a simple thanks!? YOU ONLY HARASS AND LOOK DOWN ON OTHERS!" Logan started yelling. I saw Ashlyn pop her head out from behind the wall and shake her head no. I ignored her and held my pocket knife in my hand"OH JUST SHUT UP ALREADY!" Barron grabbed a chunk of Logan's hair and Logan grabbed his arm. I did a hand movement showing Logan what to do.

He tripped him and pinned him down"GET OFF OF-" Before he could finish Logan bashed his face onto the ground. The light behind us flickered"I think it would be wise for you to start caring." I opened my knife and walked around the two

"Barron what's taking so long?" Some kids walked out"HEY GET OFF HIM!" Another kid yelled. I pulled Logan up and kicked a kid in the head. Another one came up from behind me and grabbed me. Everyone ran out. Ben slammed a kid into the ground, Taylor's hair was grabbed, Tyler was punched, and Ash kicked a kid in the head.

Aiden ran over and kicked the kid that had me so he would trip then Aiden grabbed me"You okay?" He asked"Y- AGH!" I fell to my knees and covered my ears. Aiden clearly didn't know what was wrong but he kneeled down and held his hands over my hands. "It's loud..." I whispered "What?" Aiden's voice was muffled. I looked up at a building and it was flickering...there was phantoms.

"CALM DOWN!"

The other kids ran back inside. Logan had my knife and it was bloody. "Just what was that?" Taylor asked"I'm usually not that violent..." she was shaking. I stood up slowly and Aiden made sure I was okay. "They attacked us first...We might have went overboard but they deserved it." Tyler crossed his arms"No, no that's not the problem Taylor could be right...you- you guys well we all...sounded like phantoms." I looked up from the ground and put my hand over my mouth.

"Y/N...what's wrong?" Taylor asked. I leaned over on Aiden and his eyes widened "One of them apparently had something sharp." He spun me around and lifted the back of my shirt. "That's deep." Tyler walked over. Aiden let my shirt fall back down and I leaned on him ."I'm lightheaded." I whispered "I'll carry you."

Chapter 19

"Are you guys okay...? Aiden why are you carrying Y/N?" Dad asked"Uhhhh she's tired." Aiden tilted his head. We got in the car and I put my head on Aiden's shoulder. We drove back to the house and went to the graveyard."So...you think the Phantom dimension is influencing us?" Tyler asked"No only that but...I think it's impacting the real world as well. I saw phantoms in a building window." I groaned. Ben had stitched my back.

"What do we do?" Taylor asked"Well, it all started when Logan got mad I got this like- gut feeling. But I also had this killing intent." I looked up "Maybe negative energy sets it off..." Taylor suggested "So...we need to avoid getting angry?" Logan asked"Yeah." I laid down in the seat"How do we do that if our entire situation is negative?" Tyler asked"I don't know what to do anym ore...we need to get to Savannah."

Ryan's POV

"That's what happened boss." I sighed"Hm...I see. If they have energy spikes like that they'll draw unwanted attention. How unfortunate. I was wishing to lay low a while longer. I suppose we can't always get what we want. Start making preparations." He was staring at a bird"To capture the kids?" I asked"Yes." He nodded

"What about the teacher?" I asked"What an idiotic question. He'll disappear too." He rolled his eyes

Y/N POV

A few weeks later

"I think the cooler is ready." Mom sat down

"I'll get it." Dad walked over"Hey Mike! We brought Mac and cheese." Jessica smiled. Dad started talking to Ben's parents and Lily. I was hanging on my bar."Hey girl!" Jessica walked over"Hi Jessica!" I smiled"How ya feeling birthday girl?" She asked"Good." I pointed at Ashlyn"That's my twin. The one I used to talk about on the phone with Aiden. Don't forget to tell her happy birthday." I looked over at Aiden.

"Hey." He walked over. I just smiled. "Wanna get down?" He asked"Yeah." I moved a bit so he could grab me. He helped me get down."How's your back?" He asked"It still hurts but not that bad." I put my hand on my hip

I grabbed a bowl of candy and walked over to Lil y."Want some?" I asked"Yeah!" She took a sucker"I want so-" Aiden stopped when I smacked his hand"You don't need any candy mister hyperactive." I rolled my eyes"Ashlyn do you think you could wait on the twins then bring them to the graveyard?" Mom asked"Yeah." Ashlyn nodded. We all walked out to the graveyard and I sat on the hood of a bus.

After a few minutes the twins came out. The twins put gifts and food down then Taylor yelled about a bunny. "TAYLOR!" I yelled"Y/N!" She ran over and hugged me. Aiden went to go try and catch the bunny but Ashlyn caught it. We made up last week so we weren't completely ignoring each other anymore.

Time passed by really fast."Do they not realize it's almost midnight?" Tyler asked"Guess not." I shrugged and ran my hand through Aiden's hair again. He was laying with his head in my lap."Let's go." Ashlyn stood"Ben can I see Lily for a minute?" I asked. Ben nodded and she ran over."What did you wanna tell me?" I asked"Well one, happy birthday! And two, Aiden wouldn't shut up about." She poked my forehead "Oh really?" I smiled"Yeah!" She smiled as I handed her to her mom"We're gonna go get something so we'll be right back." I smiled.

Chapter 20

I sat down on the bus seat by the door and Aiden laid his head back in my lap."You've become less of a jerk lately." Ashlyn stared at Tyler"Was that supposed to be a compliment?" He asked"I guess." Ashlyn shrugged"How much times left?" Tyler asked"2 minutes." Logan put his head on the side of his tires"I'm gonna say something cringe." I looked up"Oh yay." Tyler did jazz hands

"Just in case anything happens just know I love you guys." I leaned my head back"That wasn't cringe." Taylor laughed"Thanks Y/N." Logan smiled

Shift

Time Skip

"Is that all?" Ashlyn asked"Yup!" Aiden closed the jeep door"Alright. Let's go then." I hopped in the driver seat. The twins and Ben got in the middle while Logan and Ashlyn were in the back with our guns. "Everybody got their lights?" I asked"Yeah." Taylor nodded"You know what to do?" I looked over at Aiden"Yup." He kissed my forehead "Don't die." I smiled"I won't." He swung his knife around.

I put my foot on the gas and drove out. I heard the door slam shut.

Honk

The door to the shed that let us in the graveyard swung open then shut. Aiden jumped in and I floored it. "Are they following?" I yelled so Logan could hear me over the car"Yeah. They aren't keeping up though." Logan answered "We're driving about two hours right? To the next town?" I asked"Yeah! I know the area well." He replied

"Y/N, it's been thirty minutes can I PLEASE turn on music..." Aiden whined"Aiden I need to stay focused..." I stared at the road"When you pass the school take a right!" Logan yelled"Alright!" I yelled back.

It's smooth sailing so far. I can't even see one phantom though...it's making me feel uncomfortable.

I turned right. Why are cars everywhere...yeah it's a road but gosh. And that cliff is extremely steep."W HAT THE-" I swerved around a tree root"What was that for!?" Tyler yelled"There was a giant tree root in the road." I rolled my eyes"This roads normally fairly maintained." Logan said"Are you sure this is the right road?" I asked"Yeah I'm positive. There were never riots this way though. Ah yeah that's the gas station we usually...pass?" Logan sounded confused "That's not a good sign." Tyler mumbled"I can try and find another road..." I thought if there were any other ways that I knew about I looked up.

What the fuck is that...

"H-Hey what's with the speed!" Taylor yelled"Y/N what are you doing!?" Tyler yelled"Y/N, what's up?" Aiden looked over at me

"Something...something was in the trees." It started to get bumpy"What happened to the road?" Taylor asked"We should turn around something obviously isn't right!" Tyler shouted

"We can't!" Ashlyn yelled"Why not!?" Tyler yelled again"It's behind us..." me and Ashlyn said in sync.

Chapter 21

"There's no way our lights can do damage to that thing!" Tyler yelled"D-Do I try shooting it?" Logan asked"No! It could attract more!" I yelled

Rock pillars...

"Y/N WE NEED TO TURN AROUND BEFORE WE RUN INTO MORE!""I KNOW I KNOW!""COME ON ITS GETTING CLOSER!"

"FUCK IT!"

I drifted around the rock pillar"IS EVERYONE OKAY!?" I yelled"Yeah...doors banged up but we're fine!" Taylor yelled. Stupid roots and cars!

I swerved

Click

My eyes widened as I watched Tyler fly out of the car. "TYLER!" Taylor screamed. I kept driving forward." GO BACK!" Taylor screamed again"DO YOU GUYS TRUST ME!?" I yelled"YES!" Everyone yelled. I spun the wheel and the car was now facing the phantom."NO NO NO COME ON!" I yelled.

Tyler had already fallen and it was followed by a blood curdling scream. I started driving by the cliff praying the phantom wouldn't catch up.

I saw it.

I saw him.

I saw the tree.

Another big phantom slammed into the one behind us. "COME ON WONT YOU GO ANY FASTER!" I yelled. I AM NOT LETTING HIM DIE!

I drove down off a slope. We crashed into a tree.

Chapter 22

I looked up at the tree we had just crashed into. "OUT OF THE CAR NOW!" I yelled and jumped out. Everyone else did too."Get back. Better yet, run." I started running in the direction I saw Tyler fall.

BOOM

The car exploded.

We looked everywhere but we couldn't find him."Hey.. .Taylor it's okay." I opened the door to a small store. She sat down and leaned on Ben's shoulder.

Shift

We all stood up and I stared at Tyler. Please wake up come on!"TYLER!!" Taylor screamed while shaking him"WAKE UP WAKE UP!" Taylor yelled"WHAT DO WE DO!?" She started crying "MOM!""TAYLOR!"

Dad ran in and lifted him up"Hey! What are you doing with my son!?" Taylor's mom asked"He needs to get to the hospital!" Dad yelled. His eyes were almost fully black.

I jumped in the car

Buzz

Crazy _

CrazyTaylor's with us

You_K. Thanks.

Crazy_Dont blame yourself

You_Aiden what I did was dumb! I shouldn't have drove so recklessly!

CrazyPlease...we were being chasedby that thing! You had every right todrive like that!

You _It was still dumb! And I'm at the hospital

CrazyNo it wasn't! Also, I'm right behind you.

I jumped out of the car and followed my parents as inside. They took Tyler back and I sat on a bench. Aiden sat. Beside me and everyone else sat. It was silent.

I kept tapping my foot and looking at Taylor. "Y/N." Aiden whispered. I looked at him. He ran his hand overtop of mine"You did the best you could." He looked down at our hands"Please...stop beating yourself up over it." He looked up at me. I just stared at him before I started shaking. His eyes widened and he pulled me into a hug while slipping his hand into mine. I cried into his chest.

"Hey troop." My dad walked up and rubbed my back. Aiden looked up at him and I did too."Wanna...take a walk?" Dad asked"Mhm." I nodded and let go of Aiden's hand. He smiled at me as I stood up then looked down at his hand and stopped smiling. I watched him as I walked out the doors. He held his hand to his chest then pulled his legs up.

"So, what happened?" Dad asked"We told you in the car...we went to get Tyler's guitar then he just...collap sed." I looked at the sidewalk "Y/N. I mean what really happened." Dad looked at me.

Chapter 23

"Y/N I mean what REALLY happened.""I-We-" I looked at the ground

What really happened...? I don't know. I don't know why that woman left us there, I don't know what those creatures are, Why Ashlyn let me take the lead, How to protect them, How to escape the circle of hell we're trapped in, I don't know how to explain, I DONT KNOW!

"Listen kiddo...anything you tell me I'll believe. You have my word." He put his hand on my shoulder "We have no proof...you'll think we're on drugs or on drugs but we aren't and-" I tangled my hands in my hair"Hey, hey. Look at me. We always believe you no matter what. Me and your mom will always believe you. Do you understand?" He tilted my chin up and cupped my face.

I grabbed his wrist and started crying."It's okay." He pulled me into a hug

I explained EVERYTHING to him"So this happens every night?" He asked"Yeah." I pressed the water bottle to my head"Well, that explains your shadow." He looked at the ground"WHAT-" I sat up"Why it has short hair." He pointed "Wait but I thought you couldn't see it?" I looked over at him"I didn't. Not until we got into the hospital. When you showed us before me and your mom started to uh see creatures that sound like these "phantoms" you described." He looked over at me"Da d...we have to tell the others." I stood up"Agreed." He stood up and we ran towards the hospital."GUYS!""E MMA!"

"WE NEED TO TALK."

"Wait wait hold on...how are the parents seeing the phantoms if they didn't go to Savannah?" Logan asked"We'll figure that out later. Right now we need to focus on what to do about Tyler." Mom scratched her neck"So if I understand right, if we were to place supplies then you'd be able to use them?" Dad asked. I nodded.

"Emma, do you think you can tell the others while I take troop to town?" Dad looked at mom"I can try..." she whispered "Wait- I wanna come." Aiden got off the wall"Me too!" Logan stood and Ben did too. I walked over and pulled them all into a hug."I love you guys but you need to stay here unless Tyler wakes up. So just...call me if anything happens." I looked at Aiden when I said the last part and cupped his face"Please..." he grabbed my wrists"Aiden...you need to stay." I kissed his cheek

"Keep me updated!" I ran to catch up with dad leaving Aiden a blushing mess

"Mike buddy...what are you gonna do with all this?" Jacob asked"Sorry Jacob, tell ya later." Dad picked up the pistol"You said you guys ended up at the gas station?" Dad asked"Mhm." I hummed in response "We can't exactly leave it out in the open so we can put it in the woods." He was holding the wheel so tight his knuckles were turning whiteI kept having flashbacks to that glimpse of Tyler.

"So, I'm assuming you and Aiden are still best friend?" He asked"Yeah." I smiled"You like him?" He asked. My smile dropped "No." I shook my head"Y/N we heard you that night a while ago with Ashlyn." He rolled his eyes and laughed"He's a good kid. He'd clearly kill for you." He smiled. I just blushed."Hey troop?" Dad put his hand on my shoulder "Yeah?" I looked at him"One, it's not your fault for what happened." He squeezed my shoulder "Everyone is saying that..." I sighed"It's because it's true." He pulled his hand away

"You can date Aiden." He stopped the car

Now we debate wtf to do cause yall gonna get kidnapped and since Aiden's so hot the ceilings gonna fall for him.

Chapter 24

"Alright, this shouldn't be found." Dad put the bag down. I'm getting that same feeling I got at the arcade...

"You alright kiddo?" Dad asked"Not sure. I'm gonna call the others..." I pulled my phone out and walked off.

COME ON PICK UP AIDEN!

"Y/N?" I heard his voice on the other line "Is Tyler okay?" I asked"Yeah, he's okay. He's in rough shape though. How'd you know to call?" He asked"Oh, I got a gut feeling." I felt someone get me in a headlock "Y/N!? Y/N!?" Aiden yelled. The person stepped on my phone.

"What are you gonna do now phantom girl?" He asked. I flung my foot forward and the knife came out the end. I kicked the guy and screamed. Dad came out and grabbed me.

"WHAT THE HELL!" He yelled. He picked me up and we ran out. "He broke my phone." I held it up"Why'd you grab it then?" He asked. I pulled the case off to reveal a photo of me and Aiden in a matching outfit."Had to get this." I bucked in"Alright." Dad laughed.

The car ride back was quiet and my vision kept flickering between the two realms.

We pulled into the parking lot and I ran inside. "THANK GOD!" I was automatically attacked by Taylor and Ashlyn when I walked in."I'm fine..." I hugged them both and sat in Tyler's bed"I'm sorry..." I clenched my fists"Not your fault. Stop acting so mopey bean." He looked back at his food"What?" I held in a laugh"You wear green all the time so I'm calling you bean from now on." He mumbled "Whatever." I rolled my eyes playfully

I stood up and Aiden walked out of the bathroom. His eyes widened and he hugged me."Hey crazy." I laughed"Hey phanto." He laughed too"Phanto?" I tilted my head"Short for phantom. Just by one letter." He shrugged "About that..." I turned around and faced the others

"The whole phone thing...someone grabbed me and called me 'phantom girl'. We're being hunted or som ething..." I looked at the ground "So, stick together. I'll have the doctors." Tyler shrugged"Wouldn't that make it easier to get us?" Aiden asked"Oh...I'm not sure." Tyler looked out the window.

Chapter 25

"Alright let's move the furniture so we can be more comfortable." Aiden's mom walked to the couches "Aiden and Y/N can you get blankets from upstairs?" She asked"Yeah!" Aiden yelled and grabbed my hand. We ran up the stairs into his room to get the stuff.

Aiden kissed my cheek. I blushed and grabbed the blankets then ran downstairs.

I walked over to Ashlyn"He doesn't like that picture." I smiled"It's before I found out how fun dying my hair was." Aiden wrapped his hands around my waist"Should we play games or swim first?" He looked over at the others"What kind of games?" Taylor asked"Hey Ash, Y/N what kinda food do you want?" Dad yelled

Time skip

"Okay...I think everyone has the gist of the situation." Mom was shaking"This is crazy..." Jessica pressed her wine glass to her head"Agreed..." her husband buried his head into his hands"So the Tyler boy...has a tree in him but he isn't dead? Well...at least not here." He put his head down"We don't know." I shook my head"Maybe I'd one dies a close is made." Aiden took a bite of his pizza"Or, assuming souls are a thing, what if we're separated from our physical bodies so we don't die from physical injuries." Logan shrugged "If that's the case why do phantoms chase us then?" Taylor asked"Let's just focus on the hard facts for now. We can figure out hypotheticals later." Dad looked at Taylor.

"If spiky hair has a really big splinter dad can pull it out. He makes it not hurt! He uses a knife so it's a little scary but, it doesn't hurt." Lily smiled"Lily I said you could stay in here if you kept your headphones in." Her mom stood up"But I wanna help!" Lily put her tablet down"The monsters scared me but I'm ready now! I'll beat them up cause I'm strong like bubba!" She stood up and kicked Ben making him spit out his food

"You can take her to the playroom if you want. We'll catch you up later." Aiden's mom smiled"That's probably best. Thanks Jess." Lilys mom started walking"She was right though. If Tyler's still alive and on that tree it's gonna be really painful to get him off...they need something like a sedative just in case." Mom sat up"How are we gonna get that?" Daniel asked"We might be able to take care of that." Logan's grandpa spoke up"I'll make a few phone calls. Where was the bag?" He stood up"How are you gonna get sedatives?" Dad asked"That doesn't really matter as long as they are acquired, the tree situation can be resolved right?" Logan's grandpa shrugged "I'll send you a screenshot of the location." Dad stood up

"While he does that, we need to figure out how to keep the kids safe from the 'centipede-ish' monster." Ben's mom spoke up"I-I think I have an idea for that." Ben's dad looked up

I called Tyler and explained what we were gonna do

"That's the plan?" He asked"Yeah, for now." I nodded"And your sure the power will work?" He looked back at Logan"I mean...in theory the generator for the graveyard worked so, this should too." Logan looked at the carpet "What do you think?" Taylor asked"Well, it's the only real plan we have so, guess it's worth a shot." Tyler shrugged"I still say you guys leave me behind. I already died once what's the worst that can happen?" He asked

"Tyler we aren't doing that!" I yelled"Listen to me. We don't know what the phantoms are doing and I don't think it's as simple as killing us. We won't risk anything till we know more." I made sure I didn't yell that time"And the stroke from shock could have killed you!" I yelled again"Okay, okay, stop yelling bean." He rolled his eyes"Anyway, try to sleep before midnight." He put the phone down"Alright..." I hung up and just stared at my phone "He's right troop." Dad put his hand on my head"You kids need to sleep. We have some melatonin gummies. Well stay awake in case anything happens." Dad held a container up"Thanks dad." Ashlyn took the container "No problem kiddo." Dad smiled

"Dad...can we talk?" I looked up at him"Of course." He held his hand out and I took it. We walked over to the table with pictures on it so no one could hear us.

"When I was born...can you tell me what happened that day?" I looked up at him"You wanna know?" He asked"Mhm." I hummed in response "Alright...well, we were driving to the hospital but it was still to far away. I stopped at this abandoned school type thing so your mom could you know, have you. After she did one of the 'phantom' things was behind me. The scar on my face, it's from it grabbing me." He traced the scar with his finger "They were spawn camping me and Ash?" I tried to lighten the mood"Yup." Dad laughed a little "Now go lay down." He smiled.

I walked over to the others and laid under the blanket between Aiden and Ashlyn. I grabbed a pillow off the couch and hugged it then started crying. Ashlyn scooted over and hugged me and held one of my hands"It's okay..." she whispered and pulled the pillow out from between us. I felt a pair of hands wrap around my waist and then grab my other hand.

"You're okay..." Aiden squeezed my hand. I heard the other three crying and sat up"Taylor, Ben, Logan, come here." I whispered. They all scooted over and we were all pretty much cuddling each other.

Come on guys...we can last a little longer.

I buried my face into Aiden's chest hoping for some kind of comfort.

Shift

I stood up and ran out of the store"Hey wait up!" Taylor yelled. I stopped so she could catch up."Aiden carry this." I threw the bag at him and gave Logan the pis tol."Logan shoot only if you have to." I ran to the cliff where I saw Tyler fell.

"This is a dumb idea so I'm gonna do it first." I walked over to the edge and put my foot on the ground right under it"Don't you dare." Ashlyn started to walk over"Weeeeeeeee" I slid down the hill

"Okay! It's safe!" I yelled. I waited on them all to get down then ran. I kicked a phantom "Tyler are you-" I stopped when blood dripped on my face"Phanto! where are you?" Aiden walked around a tree"Oh, there you are." He stopped. I ran over to him"Where's the syringe?" I dug through the bag"What's wrong?" He looked up. I grabbed the syringe and we sat the latter up."Are you steady?" Aiden was holding the latter"Y-Yeah." I stuttered

"We're gonna get you down okay..." I put the syringe in Tyler's arm"Okay..." he coughed. I climbed down and Aiden grabbed me. It's a lot worse than it looks from above...

We built a contraption to get Tyler down. "You got him?" I looked over at Ben and he nodded"Another phantom..." Logan held his gun up and shot it"Let's hurry, more phantoms are showing up. We need to get to the school." Ashlyn started to walk.

Milton Keynes UK
Ingram Content Group UK Ltd.
UKHW030742121124
451094UK00013B/1050

9 798330 514946